Amazon Verified Re

"Really good recipes, without having to track down hard to find ingred[ients in your] pantry and end up with a healthy and tasty meal. Great job Cooking Dude!" —Foodrah

"Received right away and looked at recipes and sounds yummy. My son is a chef and he WANTS to try them. That is wonderful to hear for a cookbook." – Lisa

"This cookbook by John Choisser is full of great Mexican recipes. The Charro Chimichinga and the Dude's refried beans are great." -- Bernie

"This book has authentic recipes and easy to understand instructions. More importantly, it is a cookbook WITH PICTURES OF THE DISHES. I love Mexican cuisine and I find these scratch recipes authentic and easy even for the novice cook. In fact the amateurish photography is the only reason that I gave it 4 instead of 5 stars but I know that it is being picky. Please sir, write some more cookbooks and make them longer and more expensive the next time." –Marriage Coach 1

"I love that the author sat down, typed up some of the recipes that he is probably hounded for at every dinner party he gives, right down to the quick breakfast he tosses together. I love that he was able to get "secret" recipes from various favorite local restaurants all over the Southwest region. OMG, so many recipes and variations to try. A must for anyone who loves ordering Mexican but doesn't feel they could ever make a dish taste "restaurant" professionally made. With this unique cookbook you'll be able to do just that!" –Mamabear Cherei

"I love pintos and always am looking for just the right recipes for my favorite Mexican delights. Cooking Dude nails it. He's taken the time to perfect the recipes and he explains them in an easy to understand way - I already can't wait to make my own enchilada sauce! Try this book!" –P. Davis

"Witty and culturally correct written Mexican recipes. Keep writing them & I'll keep cooking them." –Love It

"Lots of recipes that my family will definitely be trying, I love that the author added pics of the finished dish! My whole family absolutely loves .Mexican food that we will use these recipes again and again! Thanks John for writing this book, love it!" –Joy

"Can't wait to try these recipes!!!! This book is interesting, informative and makes your mouth water. Thanks for letting us in on all your secrets. I will recommend this book to anyone who loves Mexican food." – Kindle Customer

"Cooking dude has a nice way of adding personality to his recipes. I absolutely love Mexican food and his recipes are fantastic!" –315 Products

"Basic, quick and delicious recipes. Fish Tacos now a family favorite. Stock you pantry for any of these recipes for a quick meal or a party spread." –Guppychef

"Finally an authentic Mexican cookbook! Simple enough for beginners. Reminds me of my favorite Mexican restaurants! I would recommend it to everyone!" – Anon.

"Just received this book and looked at all the recipes. I can't wait to try them all. I love Mexican food, but live in Small Town Alabama and I don't have access to real authentic Mexican food." -- mhm63"

"This cookbook was exciting to read, informative and fun. We are heading to Tucson in March and I am excited to go to El Charro. I like how the book is relaxed in the way it is written, I feel as I know the author and his friends and family. I'll be adding your cookbook to my favorites, to use as we begin our adventure to the southwest in our 5th wheel trailer to escape the cold Midwest winter. Cheers!" –Reading Gypsy

"Say Ole! to this cookbook! Simple ingredients! Why go out for Mexican when John's recipes are "muy facil!"(very easy) and "muy delicioso! "(very delicious!) The Cooking Dude Gringo -- deserves a ringo!!!" – C. Walker

Mexican Food

by the

Cooking Dude

Learn to Cook Real Mexican Food

John P. Choisser

www.cookingdude.com

Photo: Green Chile and Egg Casserole

Copyright © 2012-2019 John P. Choisser

All Rights Reserved

ISBN: 9781095782903

Published by Readerplace Books, LLC

www.readerplace.com

www.cookingdude.com

www.johnchoisser.com

Published in the U.S.A.

Dedication

To my grandmother Sue (Ja-Ja) Jackson and mother Eda Choisser for encouraging me to learn to cook. And to my kids, Cindy, Susie, Chris, and Craig who loved our family recipes, which encouraged me to start the Cooking Dude web site so we could find what we wanted any time and any place.

Preface

Many years ago, I decided to create a web site so I could put my recipes where I could find them. As the site grew, it became apparent that there were lots of you out there who needed help cooking, so I added some tutorials and more preparation details. When you think about it, most kids don't grow up in the kitchen with their mom and grandma anymore. So I spent a little extra time describing how to cook, in addition to the recipes. In this new edition, I have also included some handy tips for using an Instant Pot or Ninja Foodi (my favorite). In a few cases, I refer to a recipe that is on Cooking Dude but not in this book. However, in the eBook version, there is usually a link to the appropriate page on the site.

It makes me happy when I receive emails from young families thanking me for freeing them from take-out and fast food dependence. A single mom feels much better about how she feeds her kids now that she can prepare her own meals, needing sometimes to actually cook only a few times a week by cleverly using leftovers. You'll notice that I rarely use exotic ingredients, and even then suggest work-arounds if they cannot be eliminated entirely.

Today, I expect you'll find the ingredients in lots more places than in the past. I'm from Arizona originally, and grew up on Sonoran style Mexican food. I notice the difference here in San Diego, but there are some positives – fish tacos started here. But when I was in the Air Force, those of us from the West had serious Mexican food withdrawal symptoms. One night a friend of mine called to invite us over for a Mexican feast. He had flown in from Colorado with fresh tortillas, dried pinto beans, fresh Anaheim chiles, and a case of Coors beer. He was flying an F-4 Phantom jet fighter, and I could understand stashing everything except the beer. It turns out that he had to leave his parachute in Colorado and sit on the beer all the way home. Well, if the airplane stopped flying for some reason, at least he had plenty of beer to drink on the way down…

The Cooking Dude series of Kindle and print books is intended to extract some material from the Cooking Dude web site to cut down on the time you need to find recipes, and to add new material that is not yet on the site. The site also provides additional "how-to" tips that won't fit in the book. But mainly, the book provides a means to reach far more people than the site can.

I started cooking once I was tall enough to reach the stove top, and have enjoyed it ever since. Many of the recipes that I have developed over the years have turned into family favorites, and both the site and these books have made it easier for my kids and grandkids (and lots of friends) to find and cook the things they like.

When others have contributed ideas and recipes, I try to give appropriate credit. Some of the recipes have interesting historical connections, or an unusual back story, and I include them, as well. I also get lots of emails from users, and you are welcome to send me comments, corrections, and ideas.

I also recommend that in addition to the paperback version of this book for your kitchen, you also keep the eBook version in your smart phone to have while you're shopping. Oh, and don't delete the first eBook version, because some of those recipes have been replaced by new ones.

I hope you enjoy the books. But mostly, I hope you enjoy cooking and eating!

The Cooking Dude, John P. Choisser, San Diego, California, USA

Table of Contents

Dedication 3
Preface 5
Table of Contents 6
Cooking Dude Pinto Beans (Frijoles de Olla) 8
    Barbeque Beans 9
Juan's Refried Beans (Refritos) 10
    Chicarrónes 10
Drunken Beans (Frijoles Borrachos) 11
El Vaquero's Cowboy Beans (Frijoles Charro) 12
Fernando's Queso Fundido 13
Traditional Mexican Rice 14
Craig's Foodi Carnitas 16
Mexican Corn 18
Cooking Dude's Guacamole 19
Mama's Tortilla Soup 21
El Charro Chimichangas 23
    Multi-cooker 24
Easy Quesadillas 25
    El Centro Fried Quesadillas (Quesadillas Especial) 26
        Multi-cooker 27
Jalapeño Peanut Butter Boats 28
Juanito's Enchilada Sauce 29
Dude's Enchiladas 31
    Avocado Salad 32
Green Chile Casserole 33
    Instant Pot or Ninja Foodi Chile Casserole Shortcut 35
John's Mexican Red Sauce 37
    Multi-cooker 38
Tacos, Folded and Rolled 39
    Multi-cooker 41

- Cabo Carne Asada Tacos and Carne Asada 42
- San Diego's Fish Tacos 45
  - Multi-cooker 46
- Chiles Rellenos de Foodi 47
- Shrimp Vera Cruz 49
- Chicken Loco 52
- About the Author 54
- Prologue 55

Cooking Dude Pinto Beans
(Frijoles de Olla)

There must be a million bean recipes. Maybe a billion. Anyhow, I've tried and collected dozens myself trying to get the taco shop bean flavor, and finally I'm darn close. If I come across an improvement, you'll be the first to hear about it. OK, here's a News Flash. As you will see below, using your Instant Pot or Ninja Foodi can cut the cooking time down to an hour, even without an overnight soak!

The beans always start out as pot beans, or in Spanish, frijoles de olla. Now these beans are plenty good by themselves, and we eat them lots of ways. They also can easily be turned into cowboy beans (or frijoles caballero), barbeque beans, drunken beans (frijoles borrachos), refried beans, or used in chili. In the photo above, I'm serving the beans right out of the pot with some grated cheese. (Along with New York Steak Arrachera.)

Contrary to the first two million recipes for pinto beans, you don't have to soak them first overnight. You also don't have to do the "quick soak" method, which brings them to a boil and then has you let them sit there for an hour. No, mi amigo, if they can do it this way in Tucson and Cabo Mexican restaurants, that's good enough for me. Rinse 'em and cook 'em. (Those of you who live at higher altitudes are used to the fact that your boiling water isn't as hot as mine, and cooking usually takes longer.) It does seem like soaking first will result in plumper beans, except with pressure cooking. But even when I'm using the pressure mode of the Ninja Foodi, I still soak the beans for an hour or two if I have time. Of course, we're talking about starting with dried pintos, but if you need to use canned, this recipe will give you some ideas about doctoring them up.

I've seen and tried recipes for pintos that include lots of ingredients and vice versa. But here's the winner, in my opinion:

Sort through the beans as you add them to the pot, looking for and discarding the little pieces of New Mexico soil and pebbles that are usually included in the bag as little gifts from the Southwest. Swish the beans around in the water to clean them off, and then drain the rinse water. Here's what's in the pot that goes on the stove:

> 1 pound (2 cups) dried pinto beans
> 1 head (yes, head, not clove) garlic, chopped
> 1 medium onion, chopped
> 3-4 oz. salt pork (about ¼ package) rind removed, cut in small dice (optional)
> 1 teaspoon dried epazote leaves (optional)
> 8 cups water (2 1/2 cups for Instant Pot)
> salt and pepper

If you are using an Instant Pot, Ninja Foodie, or other pressure cooker, I recommend that you cut the amount of garlic and onion in half. Pressure cooking, which is for a short time, compared to simmering for hours, tends to leave much more of the flavor in, resulting in too much garlic and onion flavor in the beans for my taste.

The epazote is optional, but if you've got a market in the area that sells it, use it. It adds a flavor you can't get any other way. Sometimes you see cilantro called for as a substitute, but it's not even close.

OK, now you've got the pintos in the water on the stove and you're standing there with a whole head of garlic in your hand wondering what to do next. Here's what you do: cut the top off the garlic, and tear the head apart into individual cloves. Now peeling each clove is easy if you first cut off the root end and smash the clove under the side of your knife, giving the knife a gentle bash with your fist, if necessary. Now the peel and the garlic part ways easily, so you can chop the pile of garlic and dump it in the pot.

If you are using an Instant Pot or Ninja Foodi, add a teaspoon of salt and pepper now, add water to cover the beans by one inch, close it up, make sure the relief valve is closed, and set it to High Pressure for 45 minutes. If you have time to soak the beans, make sure the water covers the beans by ½ inch or so when you start cooking. The pressure cooking will use less than the eight cups of water because very little is lost as steam during cooking. If they are too watery, just switch to sauté or simmer mode to boil off some more water.

If you're using a pot on the stove, stir them once in a while, and after a while the onion, garlic, and epazote will vanish. The pot needs to simmer for three hours or so, so you can keep the heat pretty low, or even use a crock pot and let them cook all day. Toward the end of the cooking time add salt and pepper. Taste the beans, and when they're tender and yummy, they're done.

Depending on the temperature and your altitude, you may need to add some water, or if too watery, boil a little longer to thicken the beans.

Serve them with the garnish(s) of your choice: cilantro, shredded cheese, salsa, catsup (what? yep, the kids love that), Tabasco, chopped onion... you get the idea. Save the leftovers for later in the week, or better yet, make *Refried Beans* (see below) out of them.

Barbeque Beans

Make the pot beans and add your favorite BBQ sauce. Boy, this is a tough one....

Juan's Refried Beans (Refritos)

To turn the pintos into Refried Beans, put them in a skillet and warm them up. If you started with a pound of beans, add a 1/4 cup of melted lard or bacon fat (the lard is best) and stir. Add more and stir more. Some Mexican cooks then finish off with some canned (condensed) milk to give them that wonderful rich taste and light brown color. How much lard and milk is up to you, and depends also on how many beans you started with. Start with 1/4 cup of lard and 1/2 cup of milk per pound of beans. Omit the milk if you wish, and don't be afraid to experiment. But if you've ever eaten good refried beans, you'll know it when you get there. In the photo above, I've melted grated Mexican Blend cheese over the beans before serving. Or you can use Jack and Cheddar, or some of the authentic Mexican cheeses if you're lucky enough to live near a Mexican market (which is also where you might find epazote).

Chicarrónes

For the ultimate flavor, render your own pork fat, and use instead of lard. You'll need about 1/3 pound of fat, which your butcher may sell you for $1 a pound, or maybe free. Slice the fat into strips, and put in a sauce pan with a little water. Heat it up and boil off the water. Let the crackling begin... After a while, you'll have the chitlins floating around in the liquid fat. When they have rendered all the fat they can, scoop them out with a slotted spoon onto a paper towel and lightly salt them. Now you've got some chitlins to munch on while you stir the fat into the beans. I hope heaven is this good...

By the way, the chitlins are called chicarrónes in Mexico, and besides being a great munchie are used in Frijoles Charro (see below).

Of course, you can sauté the fat in your Instant Pot or Ninja Foodi, also. I'm sure it can also be done in an air fryer, or in the Fry Mode in a Foodi, as well.

Drunken Beans (Frijoles Borrachos)

4 strips of thick smoky bacon
1 small white onion, chopped
1 jalapeño pepper, seeded and diced
1/4 cup tequila
salt
cilantro, chopped for garnish

Frijoles borrachos start with the pot beans, with one exception. Add two strips of thick-cut smoked bacon chopped up when you make the pot beans. (You'll probably like this so much you'll do it every time for all the bean recipes.) If you've already made the beans, just cook 8 strips of the chopped bacon, sauté the veggies, and then add the beans.

Otherwise, when the beans are nearly done, fry another four strips of bacon, chopped up, until nearly crisp. Remove the bacon, and all but two or three tablespoons of the bacon fat. Add the chopped onion and jalapeño and fry for about 10 minutes. Dump the mixture into the beans with the cooked bacon, and re-heat the beans. If the beans are too watery, just simmer them uncovered for a while but don't forget to stir them. If they stick to the bottom of the pot and char you'll have a lot more smoky taste than you want!

Oh, by the way, the tequila adds a wonderful flavor, but despite the name Drunken Beans, there won't be much alcohol left at serving time. But you can sip it while making the beans…

El Vaquero's Cowboy Beans (Frijoles Charro)

There used to be a restaurant in Cabo San Lucas called El Vaquero. Their chef, Fernando Palomino Baluaceda, taught me how to make this dish, plus the Queso Fundido.

For this recipe you'll need to make the chicarrónes, described above, plus a pot of Frijoles de Olla.

2 lbs. pinto beans, cooked
4 strips bacon
1 cup chopped onion
2 cups chopped tomato
1/2 cup chopped cilantro
1 1/2 cup chicarrónes (fried pork rinds)
1/4 cup diced Serrano chiles

Fry the bacon until done, and add the remaining ingredients except for the pinto beans. Fry the vegetables in the bacon fat until tender, and add the chicarrónes. Fry another few minutes, and add the beans along with some of their cooking liquid. Simmer for 15 minutes or so. Serve in bowls.

Fernando's Queso Fundido

While we were there, chef Fernando also showed us how he makes Queso Fundido. This was a great appetizer, which we all enjoyed. Although Fernando baked this dish in the coals of his wood fire, most of us will probably use our ovens at home. I suggest that baking in a 350 degree F oven for 20 minutes to melt the cheese and blend the flavors. You might also experiment by adding a few drops of liquid smoke to add Fernando's smoky touch. An Air Fryer or Ninja Foodi also makes a good oven substitute.

Here's how to make Queso Fundido:

1 pound chorizo sausage
1/2 pound grated Monterey cheese

Fry the chorizo until done, and break it up into small pieces. Layer the chorizo and cheese in a small crock and bake until the cheese is melted.

Fernando also made a batch of refried beans. Then we sat down to a nice array of fresh salsas, cold beer, the fundido, the frijoles charro, and had a party!

Traditional Mexican Rice

    This Mexican rice recipe is better than any other I've tried so far. The flavor is outstanding, and the colors and textures make any dish you serve it with look better.

    This makes enough for six or seven servings, so you might have some left over. If so, that's a bonus, because it can accompany some other dish another night.

    I made this dish the other night to go with chimichangas, and used Ro-Tel Diced Tomatoes with Lime Juice and Cilantro. That made the recipe even better.

    I got some fresh peppers from my garden, and wound up with two Poblanos and one jalapeño. They give a little special flavor to the dish at the end, and can be used as garnish. However, I found that the jalapeño was tender and sweet after spending ten minutes in the rice, and was delicious and not too hot to eat along with the rice.

    1 cup long grain white rice
    7 or 10 ounce can of chopped tomatoes, with juice, preferably Ro-Tel
    1/2 onion, chopped
    3 garlic cloves, chopped
    2 tablespoons oil
    2 cups chicken stock
    1/2 teaspoon salt
    3 fresh green chiles, such as Poblano or Anaheim, maybe one of them a jalapeño
    1 cup frozen peas, or one 8 ounce can
    black pepper
    cilantro

Put the rice in a bowl and cover with boiling water and let stand for 10 minutes. Pour the rice into a strainer, rinse, and let sit to drain for a while.

Pour the tomatoes, garlic, and onion into a blender and process until smooth. Here you can use a blender, food processor, or an electric hand blender (boat motor) in a bowl. Or if you don't have any of these just leave them mixed as-is.

Heat the oil in a large sauce pan, and add the rice. Stir the rice to distribute the oil. Let the rice cook undisturbed for five minutes, stir, and repeat. After 10-15 minutes the rice should be light brown and smell great.

Add the tomato mixture and stir for three or four minutes to absorb the liquid. Add the stock, salt, chiles, and peas if you are using frozen. If you are using canned peas, wait until the end to add them. Continue to cook, stirring frequently, another ten minutes or so until the liquid has been absorbed and the rice is tender. (Your mouth will know when it's done.)

Take the pan off the heat, cover it, and let it stand for another ten minutes or so. When it's time to serve, remove the chiles, fluff up the rice, and enjoy!

Craig's Foodi Carnitas

My youngest son Craig, author of the famous book *Great Recipes to Pair with Shitty Wine – Wine Pairing for Cheap People,* has a Ninja Foodi like mine. He is also having a blast inventing new ways to do things, and his carnitas recipe is really good.

He started with a 2-3 pound frozen pork shoulder from Costco, and cut it into pieces. He recommends cutting it up into two-inch pieces. He put the meat into the Foodi, and added a jar of Herdez green tomatillo sauce and a cup of chicken stock. He then used the Pressure Mode of the Foodi to cook the meat for about 40 minutes. He drained the sauce out and browned the meat using the Broil Mode. After de-fatting the sauce, he added the sauce back into the meat and finished shredding it.

He thinks that squeezing an orange and lime into the meat, along with a little more salt, might improve the dish a little. Felicia, our social media guru, adds fresh orange juice and dried oregano to her carnitas, and gets rave reviews.

He served the carnitas tacos with soft corn tortillas, avocado, and grated hard Mexican cheese. Adding more salsa or hot sauce is up to you.

Mexican Corn

    You can prepare this either on your outdoor (or indoor) grill, maybe while you are grilling something else, or you can make it in your air fryer or Ninja Foodi, like the corn shown in the photo. It's really simple, but delicious as any of you who have had this from the Mexican food vendors on the streets of Tijuana can attest. The details are up to you, but some vendors I have talked to have different versions. Most often, the corn is coated with either mayonnaise, or a mixture of yogurt and mayo. Sometimes some adobo sauce is in the mix, which is really good. Then the corn is sprinkled with chili powder and hard grated cheese and grilled until there are a few black spots here and there on the corn. Dress it up with some chopped cilantro, and you have a real corny treat! I was out of Mexican cheese, so I used Parmesan. Worked great!

Cooking Dude's Guacamole

One of the delights of living in Southern California is that not only do we produce most of the nation's avocados, we also consume most of them. And I try to do my share. I usually serve them as guacamole with tortilla or potato chips, or with taquitos (rolled tacos) and refried beans as shown in the photo.

There are lots of recipes for guacamole, and you'll find them pretty easily without looking very hard. But around here, we don't do some of the things others do.

For starters, we don't add mayonnaise, sour cream, or other things that stretch the quantity. Yes, it saves money, and avocados are expensive, but if you're going to spend the buck, why not enjoy the full flavor? So we just use avocados and seasonings.

I prefer the Hass variety, and the commercial growers have been steadily replacing the Fuerte and other varieties with Hass. Hass is available year-round now, and ships well because it has a thicker skin than other varieties.

The fruit is ripe when it darkens from green to nearly black, and yields gently to a squeeze. Run a knife around the fruit starting at the stem end, cutting through to the seed. Then twist the two halves in opposite directions, and they will come apart with the seed stuck in one of the halves. Whack the seed with the knife, give it a twist, and the seed comes free.

Now with a knife without a sharp point, you can score the meat of the fruit up and down and back and forth, so when you scoop it out with a spoon, it's already diced.

Mash the avocado in a bowl. Then mix the following:

3 or 4 avocados
1/2 teaspoon garlic salt
juice from one whole lemon
2 teaspoons Tabasco

Now you can modify this to your own taste. You can change the quantities listed above, and maybe make some of these additions, as shown in the next photo:

diced jalapeño pepper
lime juice
onion powder
diced tomato
diced olives
chopped cilantro
diced onion, or green onion

All these things are good, just don't get so carried away that you can't taste the avocado anymore!

Mama's Tortilla Soup

     In our house, this is the substitute for chicken noodle soup. Mrs. Cooking Dude swears that this soup is not only delicious, but kills viruses and bacteria. Maybe so, and if you really need to clear out your sinuses, just increase the white pepper.

     This is basically a chicken broth soup, with Mexican and Southwest flavorings and fried tortilla strips instead of noodles. The tortilla strips can either be made from flour tortillas or corn tortillas, and if you don't want to make them, use tortilla chips out of the bag.

     The garnishes really make it special. I normally serve it with a wedge of lime, chopped cilantro, avocado slices, and a hard, white grated cheese, either Mexican or Parmesan.

     I keep a bag of chicken tenders or boneless chicken breast pieces in the freezer for lots of uses, and this soup is one of them. Many times I make this soup on the spur of the moment because it's both good and fast. This can also serve as a simple but flavorful company dish if you need to come up with food for visitors all of a sudden.

     Fortunately, we also nearly always also have on hand either flour or corn tortillas (or both). If we have uncooked flour tortillas, so much the better, because in addition to the tortilla strips, I can also make fried quesadillas to go with the soup. Of course, with cooked flour tortillas, I can always make regular quesadillas, which are also a quick lunch, breakfast, dinner or appetizer, with or without meat.

     Here's how you make Tortilla Soup for four:

6 cups chicken broth, canned, instant, or home-made
5 or 6 pieces of chicken tenders or breasts, thawed and cubed, or two whole breasts, cubed
1 teaspoon cumin

1 teaspoon chili powder
1 tablespoon vegetable oil
1 teaspoon butter
1 cup chopped onion
1 celery stalk, chopped
1 large or 2 small carrots, chopped
3 tablespoons flour
2 cups chopped tomatoes
3 cloves garlic, minced, or 1 tablespoon garlic purée
2 four-ounce cans chopped green chiles
1/2 teaspoon white pepper (add more before serving, if desired. But taste first -- this is the heat!)
lime wedges
chopped cilantro
avocado slices
grated hard cheese, Mexican or Parmesan

Start heating up the broth, cumin, and chili powder in a pot, and add the cubed chicken. While that is heating up, heat the oil and butter in a skillet.

When the butter and oil are hot, add the chopped onion, celery, and carrot, and cook for a few minutes, stirring frequently. After three or four minutes, add the garlic, tomatoes, and green chiles. Cook for another three or four minutes, and add the flour. Stir to incorporate the flour and cook for another minute or two.

Then add some broth to the skillet, a little at a time. As it thickens, add more broth to make a paste. Then add it all back to the pot with the chicken, and stir to thicken. Let it simmer for fifteen or twenty minutes, covered, to let the flavors meld.

Meanwhile, fry the tortilla strips, make the quesadillas or fried quesadillas, or open the tortilla chip bag. Yes, you may use tortilla chips out of the bag in the soup; if they are very large you may want to crumble them. Bagged tortilla chips are normally made from corn tortillas, which is fine. You can also fry your own from cut up fresh corn tortillas.

This has to be the most delicious health food in the world!

El Charro Chimichangas

Chimichangas were invented in Tucson at the El Charro Cafe. This cafe, now in more than one location, is the oldest Mexican restaurant in the U.S. under continuous operation by the same family. It was founded in 1922, and if you're ever in Tucson, don't miss it.

My mom and dad both graduated from the University of Arizona, and dated at the original restaurant, sometimes with my grandmother. Although we now live in San Diego, during a recent trip to Tucson we dined there with my grandchildren. That makes five generations of my family that have eaten there (but not all at once!).

Chimichangas are a real taste treat! They are actually deep-fried burritos, usually filled with refried beans. If you don't have a deep fryer, it doesn't matter much; just heat 1/2 or so of oil in a skillet and cook them there. It's a little slower because they only cook on one side at a time, but they taste just as good!

I normally include chopped onion and shredded Mexican cheese with the beans, and you can experiment with other fillings, including jalapeños, chopped lettuce, salsa, and so forth.

Chimis are great either for dinner or as an appetizer. We make them from uncooked flour tortillas. The tortillas we buy for home are smaller than the big ones at the taco shops, so one or two as an appetizer is not too much.

The important thing is to keep the insides inside while frying. To do this, spread the filling over the middle half of the tortilla about 1/3 the way down the tortilla. Then fold over the part nearest you, fold in the two sides, and roll the tortilla up.

After the final roll-up, moisten the edge and press together lightly. Let them dry out a little to seal them up. You can see step-by-step photos on cookingdude.com.

Now they are ready for frying. They will only take a couple of minutes, so keep an eye on them. Since they cook so quickly, I only cook two or three at a time so they have plenty of room in the fryer. After frying, drain the fryer basket for a few seconds, and dump the chimis out onto a wire rack over paper towels. When they are cool enough to handle, it's chow time!

Multi-cooker

Easy Chimichangas are a natural for the Ninja Foodi or your air fryer. No hot oil, no smelling up the house, and so fast and easy you can make just one and it's worth the effort.

Start with a corn tortilla, and put some beans, onion, and cheese after you lightly spray both sides of the tortilla with cooking spray. The spray not only softens the tortilla so it rolls up more easily, but it also adds crunch to the finished product.

Then roll it up, tucking in the ends, and place it in the air fryer. Cook at 380-390 for about 7 minutes, checking once in a while, because all cookers are not alike, and the time also depends on where the chimi is place in the cooker. The result is a delicious crunchy chimi. Someone took a bite out of this one before I had a chance to take the photo.

Easy Quesadillas

    This is probably the number one quick snack around here. But we also frequently make them for breakfast, appetizers, or a fast lunch.

    You can either start with cooked or uncooked flour tortillas. I usually prefer the uncooked, but for quesadillas it doesn't make much difference.

    It can't get much easier than this: heat up the griddle or large frying pan, put in a tortilla, wait for it to cook (if it's raw), turning several times, sprinkle grated cheese over one half, fold it, and wait a minute or two. Flip it over for another minute and it's done.

    Sometimes we also add jalapeños. You can also add cooked chicken shreds, or chopped tomato, onion, and/or green chiles. All these are great. You can also season the finished quesadilla with salt, Tabasco, Herdez or Ortega salsa (red or green), or whatever else you like.

    Experiment and enjoy. If you're a beginning cook, make this your first project!

El Centro Fried Quesadillas (Quesadillas Especial)

OK, another story here. In the January, the Blue Angels train and get ready for the coming year in El Centro, California. We got to go over there for the "graduation" of the new team because one of my daughter's sorority sisters had married a man who became one of the pilots. It turns out that the Angels' favorite Mexican restaurant is Celia's, in El Centro.

Celia's has a deep-fried special quesadilla that's worth a special trip to eat. We started timing our trips to Arizona so we would have lunch there, munching on special quesadillas, of course.

I'm not making this up, as a famous comedian used to say: One day I was getting a haircut here in San Diego, and we were discussing the coming Christmas holidays. My barber said she was going home to El Centro to visit family. I asked her if she had been to Celia's, and --are you ready? -- she said that it was owned by her aunt and uncle.

I had to suppress my evil grin as I asked her how to make the famous quesadillas, and she said that she hadn't actually worked in the restaurant's kitchen, but here's what they did at home:

The key is to start with uncooked flour tortillas. Well, we just happen to have those at home already. You spread the cheese over half, leaving a margin around the whole circle, moisten the edge, and fold over to seal. After the seal dries, you can fry the quesadillas without the cheese getting in the oil. If the tortillas you are using don't seal well with water, use egg white.

This photo shows the quesadillas ready for cooking. They are large enough so I can't use my deep fryer, so I just heat about 1/2 inch of oil in a large skillet.

Fry the quesadillas a minute or two on each side. The bubbling will stop when it's time to turn them or take them out. Then we cut them up with a pizza cutter (or quesadilla cutter) and serve.

You can use won ton skins to make a smaller version for another delicious appetizer. Don't overlook the possibility of putting some extras inside, like jalapeño slices!

Multi-cooker

In an air fryer or Ninja Foodi, do the same preparation, spraying the quesadilla with cooking spray before frying.

Jalapeño Peanut Butter Boats

This is one of the favorite appetizers around here, even for those who normally think jalapeños are too hot for them. The peanut butter is a perfect flavor complement to the hot sweetness of the jalapeño, and seems to remove some of the heat.

The photo shows both home-grown and pickled jalapenos, but most of the time, most people, including me, use pickled jalapeños that come in a jar or can.

Most recipe books tell you to wear rubber gloves when handling chiles, and to be on the safe side, so will I. But frankly, working with gloves on is very difficult, and if you are going to scratch an itch in your eye either with or without gloves on, you probably won't do it again. When you're finished, wash your hands with soap and water and you can scratch all you want. BTW, if you do get some juice in your eye, flushing it with water is the best remedy. If you can't get your head under the faucet, splash the water in your eye with your hand. You can clean up the mess later.

Anyhow, this is really easy. Slit the peppers lengthwise, and scrape out the seeds and the membranes the seeds are attached to. Now you can either leave them as is, or you can make them milder by rinsing them under a stream of water. Fill each one with your favorite peanut butter, and enjoy! Keep some extras on hand, because you will likely get requests for an encore.

Juanito's Enchilada Sauce

    You can probably buy enchilada sauce in a can, depending on where you live, but you quickly discover that it doesn't taste like the sauce in a restaurant. I don't know why. Once I asked the proprietor of a taco shop, and she told me that they also start with canned sauce, add a little peanut butter (!) to take the whang out of it, and maybe some garlic salt. Well, I tried, but still couldn't get what I wanted.

    Here's a fairly simple recipe that I found that works well enough for me. It has a rich base so that the chile powder doesn't overpower the taste. But it doesn't include peanut butter. Maybe next time....

    This sauce starts with a roux (pronounced roo) which is one of the French words you have to learn if you're going to cook. You make a roux before making many soups, sauces, and gravies.

    Here's the ingredient list for Enchilada Sauce:

3 tablespoons vegetable oil
3 tablespoons flour
1/4 cup red chile powder, mild
2 cups beef broth, canned, fresh, or powder mix
15 oz. can of tomato sauce
1/2 teaspoon dried oregano
1/4 teaspoon cumin
1 teaspoon garlic powder or granulated garlic
1 teaspoon sugar
1/2 teaspoon salt, or more if needed
1/4 teaspoon pepper

Heat the oil in a sauce pan until it is shimmering, but not smoking. Add the flour and stir to break up the lumps. Stir and cook several minutes until the flour turns brown -- about the color of peanut butter. Stir in the chile powder and let it cook for a minute. Now take the pan off the heat and let it cool a little, because when you add the liquid it will start to thicken quickly. Add the beef broth, tomato sauce and the spices, stir and replace on the heat. Add the spices and simmer for ten or fifteen minutes. If you're going to make enchiladas right away, leave some time for the sauce to cool some before you need to use it.

For an easier quick version for use as a tamale sauce or over eggs, see John's Mexican Red Sauce below.

Dude's Enchiladas

  Some enchiladas are stuffed with cheese, some with chicken, some with beef, some with pork, some with green chiles -- well, you get the idea. Also, some are rolled and some are flat. This recipe will teach you how to do all of these.

  Personally, I prefer chopped onion and shredded Mexican cheese for the filling, but you can do whatever you want. I also tend to make stacked enchiladas, because it is much easier and less of a mess than rolling them.

  First you need enchilada sauce, either homemade or canned. If you don't have the time or energy to make your own sauce, and you don't like the flavor of canned, a third option is to go to your nearest taco shop and buy a pint or two of their enchilada sauce.

  Enchiladas always use corn tortillas. You can buy 12 in a package, and that will make enough for 4-6 people. Shown in the photo below are two stacks in a roasting pan, six tortillas per stack. If you roll the tortillas, they will still fill the pan; just pack 'em in like sardines.

Corn tortillas won't roll without cracking, so they need to be heated in oil first. That also enhances their flavor, so I also do that for stacked enchiladas.

Here's a list of what you need to make enchiladas:

12 tortillas
1/4 cup or so of vegetable oil
3-4 cups of enchilada sauce
2 cups chopped onion
2-3 cups shredded cheese, preferably Mexican
1/2 cup chopped cilantro
4 oz. can of chopped olives
If desired, 1-2 cups of cooked hamburger, shredded beef, shredded chicken, or other meat filling

Preheat the oven to 350 degrees. Using a ladle, spoon some sauce in the bottom of the pan, making two circles where the tortillas are going to be. Place two tortillas side by side, spread a little sauce on them, sprinkle some chopped onion, add other filling if you wish, and add a layer of cheese. Repeat this until you run out of tortillas.

To dress up the top, add some extra sauce, cheese, chopped olives, and chopped cilantro. Bake in the oven for 30 minutes, or until heated through and the cheese is melted.

Avocado Salad

The plate shown above has refried beans and a simple avocado salad served with the enchiladas. The avocado salad is just some chopped lettuce, cherry tomatoes, olives, and some Hot Salt sprinkled over the top. It doesn't even need any dressing.

Green Chile Casserole

Technically, maybe this is a "strata" rather than a casserole. And it's not Italian. But whatever you call it, it is always a huge hit around here. I generally make it for breakfast for special occasions or when we have overnight guests. Last time I made it the compliments (and requests for the recipe) were still coming the next day.

The original recipe came from my step-daughter Lori, as I recall. I made it from memory over the next few years and accidentally changed the proportions. I ran across a hand-written version in Mom's stuff, sharing Lori's recipe with me! Full circle. Anyhow, now we have the original recipe.

Now that you can buy pre-shredded cheese (I usually buy the four-Mexican cheese blend) this is really easy. The only hard part has been grating the cheese, and now it's no longer necessary.

We normally make this with canned California Green Chiles (also called Anaheim Chiles). If you want or need to, you could use fresh chiles, and could use Poblano, which would be just as good. If using fresh chiles, however, you need to prepare them first. More about that later.

Here's what you need for Green Chile Casserole:

1 lb. can (or 2 8 oz. cans) green chiles (such as Ortega)
2 tablespoons milk
4 tablespoons flour
4 eggs
shredded or grated mixed cheeses, such as cheddar, Jack, or Mexican

Spray a 9 x9 x2 baking dish with cooking spray. Preheat the oven to 350 degrees.

Remove the chiles from the can, don't rinse, but pick off any seeds or peels you find.

Mix the milk, flour and eggs in a bowl using a fork or a whisk. A few lumps won't matter.

Tear the chiles into strips, lay them out in the dish, and sprinkle with cheese. Repeat for several layers, until you run out of chiles. The photo at below shows the second layer about to get the cheese.

Finish off with a final layer of cheese, pour over the milk, flour, and egg mixture, and put in the oven for about 1/2 hour.

In the meantime, make the sauce, prepare bacon (I'm using warmed pre-cooked bacon in the photo at top) or refried beans, if you have some on hand, and warm some tortillas.

You can use enchilada sauce, but I think that is too robust a flavor for this egg dish. I prefer to make a simple Red Sauce shown in the following recipe, which only takes a few minutes, and is delicious both on this dish, and on other things, like tamales.

When you take the casserole out of the oven, let it sit for at least ten minutes to cool off and firm up some. Slice it into serving pieces, ladle over some sauce, and get ready for the compliments!

Instant Pot or Ninja Foodi Chile Casserole Shortcut

When we had our Instant Pot, I learned make this dish for one or two very easily, and in a fraction of the time. I do the same now with my Ninja Foodi. I spray one or two small French baking dishes with non-stick spray, and then layer the chile strips and grated cheese in each one. I beat an egg or two with a teaspoon of flour and pour equal amounts into each dish.

Then I arrange the dishes in a wire caddy that fits into the Instant Pot and keeps the dishes elevated above the cup or so of water in the bottom of the pot.

Cook at High Pressure for 10 minutes, release the pressure, and remove from the pot. Let them sit for a few minutes, drizzle the Red Sauce over them, and then just place the dishes on a plate with whatever else you're serving (if anything). This is especially convenient if you've made enough red sauce to have some in the fridge already. Or use bottled salsa.

Now instead of waiting fifteen minutes for the oven to heat up, and another half hour to bake, you have prepared this elegant breakfast or brunch in fifteen minutes, have no pots or pans to wash (maybe rinse out and dry the Instant Pot), and only the serving dishes to put in the dishwasher. Well, plus the measuring cup you beat the eggs in.

John's Mexican Red Sauce

Here's a quick tomato sauce (or gravy) that is delicious over egg dishes, tamales, or chiles rellenos. It doesn't have any chile powder in it, so its flavor is different than enchilada sauce. It's also easier to make. Here's the recipe for Quick Tomato Sauce:

    1 can of tomato sauce (14 oz.)
    4 tablespoons vegetable oil
    4 tablespoons flour
    1 teaspoon garlic salt
    1/2 teaspoon dried oregano
    1/4 teaspoon dried basil
    1/4 teaspoon cumin
    1/4 teaspoon black pepper
    chopped chipotles (optional - shown in photo)

Open the can of tomato sauce and keep it handy. Heat the oil in a sauce pan until it is shimmering, and add the flour. Stir and cook until the mixture looks light brown and begins to smell toasty. (This is a "roux", pronounced "roo". You have to learn some French to cook, you know.)

Add the tomato sauce gradually, stirring constantly. You will notice that the roux thickens the sauce immediately. Fill the empty tomato sauce can with water, and add about half of it to the sauce. That's probably all you'll need, but if you made a little more or less roux, the amount of water you'll need to add will change.

Bring to a simmer, and quit adding water when the sauce is the consistency you want. Add the spices, taste, and after simmering a few minutes, add more seasonings if you wish. You can also add chopped parsley or cilantro, either to the sauce or to the finished dish as a garnish.

For smaller quantities of sauce, use the typical little 8 oz. can of tomato sauce, and reduce the other ingredients by about half. This is what I do most of the time.

Multi-cooker

In this photo, I've made the Red Sauce using the Sauté Mode of my Ninja Foodi. Then, adding a rack over the sauce, I switched to Pressure Mode to cook the tamale shown in the top photo in another six or seven minutes (depending on whether the tamale was frozen or not).

Tacos, Folded and Rolled

      Taco night is always popular at our house. They aren't much work, and they are always fun to make and to eat.

      We usually use ground beef in our tacos, but there's no reason not to use shredded beef, chicken, pork, fish, machaca, carnitas, shrimp, or just beans if you want to. Sometimes the taco's preparation changes depending on the main filling, but unless you've got taco police roaming around, go ahead and experiment with any combination you want. For an occasional special treat, I'll make Carne Asada Tacos shown in the next section. That always gets me a round of applause!

      Typically, tacos are made with corn tortillas that are either baked, fried, or just warmed. Meat tacos usually have crisp shells, made that way by frying or baking. The seafood tacos often have warmed soft tortillas, usually two layered together per taco so they don't fall apart.

      You can buy the taco shells already made, or you can purchase corn tortillas and make the shells yourself. Of course, there are pros and cons to everything. To me, the flavor of fried fresh corn tortillas is worth the extra time and effort, but I admit to often using the pre-made taco shells to save time or when I'm just lazy.

      Pre-made taco shells are cold out of the package, of course, so they need to be warmed. The easiest way is in the oven, and I usually fill them with the meat mixture and add some grated cheese before putting them in the oven. 350 degrees for 10 or 15 minutes works fine. Then as the shell warms up, the meat also warms and the cheese melts. After you add the cold ingredients, plus whatever sauce or salsa you want, you're ready to roll.

      The tacos shown in the photo had their shells fried in a deep fat fryer, which makes them very flavorful, tender, and puffy. I have a taco forming tool that holds the tortilla in the proper shape while dipping them in the oil. You can also fry them in oil in a skillet, and if they puff up too much to fold, you can poke the puffs with a long fork to let the air out. The idea is to get them fairly crispy, but not so stiff that they break when you try to fill them.

Here's a general recipe, for a dozen tacos. Feel free to experiment!

12 white or yellow corn tortillas, or 12 pre-formed taco shells
1 pound ground beef, 15%-20% fat
1 medium onion, diced*
1 medium tomato, chopped
2 cups chopped lettuce
1 cup (or more) shredded cheese (easiest to use pre-shredded Jack & Cheddar or Four Mexican cheese blend)
1 teaspoon garlic salt
1 teaspoon black pepper
1/2 teaspoon cumin
Tabasco and/or salsa (Herdez red and green salsas are the family favorite)
Parmesan (or Mexican) dry grated cheese
Chopped cilantro
Optional additional garnishes: chopped radishes, chopped olives, diced jalapeños.

* Use 1/2 for the meat mixture and 1/2 later for garnish.

Mary Ann, Mom's caregiver angel from Fiji, invented the idea of mixing all the garnishes together. The tacos in the photo were made that way. It sure speeds up the assembly line; but then everyone needs to like the same ingredients, of course.

For beef tacos, get the hamburger frying in the pan, and after some of the pink goes away, add half of the chopped onion. Stir and cook, adding the garlic salt, pepper, and cumin. After the meat is done, you can keep it warm, or even let it cool if it's going to get re-heated in the oven in the taco shells. I usually do that, even if I have fried my own shells. By the time all the shells are done, they aren't warm anymore, anyway.

This photo shows an open-faced taco made with a whole wheat tortilla. I just warmed the tortilla on a griddle for a couple of minutes and made a low-cal version that tastes great. Ms. Cooking Dude likes these, and with her favorite salsa, Herdez Green.

Traditionally, if you make seafood tacos, you not only use warm soft tortillas, but you also would use shredded cabbage instead of the lettuce. A light mayonnaise dressing, often mixed with a little yogurt, is usually added to the cabbage, and chopped fresh cilantro is a must. But don't be afraid to experiment, and if you have some tacos at a restaurant that you like, take note of the ingredients and modify your recipe.

Tacos can be served by themselves, or with a side dish of Refried Beans or Mexican Rice. Obviously, Mexican beer is probably the most popular drink, but just ice water with a lemon or lime wedge works fine. Or some Margueritas!

Multi-cooker

Use the Air Fryer mode in your Ninja Foodi if you don't have an air fryer. I use this often to make even just one or two tacos or tostadas, because it is not necessary to heat up a skillet of oil to fry the tortillas. Just spray them with cooking spray and find ingenious ways to put them in the air fryer. Here are a couple of suggestions.

In the photo on the left below, I've actually fried the taco meat in the bottom of the air fryer pan (which drains the meat as it cooks) while I fried the tortillas at the same time right above the meat. It took all of 10 minutes. Wow. Who ever heard of one-pot tacos?

Or make rolled tacos, and fry them the same way. These are ground beef and cheese:

Cabo Carne Asada Tacos and Carne Asada

Carne asada tacos are a delicious, and somewhat special, departure from our normal taco night. In this case, carne asada is used as the meat for the filling, and either corn or flour tortillas, either soft or fried, can be used for the shell.

The photo above shows a taco made with a fried flour tortilla, our local favorite, and down below is shown the more classical version with a soft warm flour tortilla and different fillings.

In our area, carne asada tacos are usually served with two small soft corn tortillas as the wrapping, with guacamole and lettuce over the meat filling. But at home, a larger crisp fried flour tortilla is the hands-down favorite.

Carne asada can also be served as a Mexican steak dinner, usually with beans, rice, and enchiladas on the side. Just follow the instructions here for the steak, and instead of cutting it up for the tacos, serve it in steak-sized pieces with the other side dishes.

Carne asada starts with either flank steak or skirt steak (preferred). In fact, in some parts of Mexico, flank steak is used for arrachera and skirt steak is used for carne asada. Either way, the meat is tenderized by pounding, and then marinated in a mixture of lime juice and spices.

Here's an easy way to fix Carne Asada Tacos or just Carne Asada:

2 pounds skirt steak, pounded and flattened with a mallet (for tacos, assume 1/4 pound per person)
1/4 cup lime juice (preferably fresh)
1 tablespoon garlic salt
1 tablespoon onion powder
1 teaspoon cumin
2 teaspoons chili powder
1 teaspoon sugar

For garnish:

Red and green bell peppers
Anaheim green chiles
White and/or red onion

For tacos:

1 flour or 2 corn tortillas per person, either warm or fried
1 avocado
1 tomato
1/2 onion, chopped
yellow or yellow/white shredded cheese
hard white cheese, either Mexican or Parmesan
salsa or hot sauce of your choice

Pound the steak to about ¼-inch thickness, and cut into pieces so they are easy to handle on the grill (like 6" x 6"). Make the marinade by mixing the other ingredients, and cover both sides of all the pieces of meat. Seal the meat in a zip lock bag and refrigerate until ready to cook. Let the meat marinate at least a couple of hours, if you can. You can include the vegetables in the marinade, if you wish.

If you're making tacos, chop the remaining ingredients for the garnish. Either warm or fry the tortillas in either a frying pan or a deep fryer. Fold the tortillas as they cook to form the taco shell.

Grill the meat over hot coals for a few minutes on each side. It's pretty thin, so it will get to medium in five minutes or less. For carne asada, serve the meat like a steak with side dishes as described above. I also like to garnish each steak with a green chile, either fresh or canned.

The more classic version starts with bell peppers and onion brushed with a little olive oil and sprinkled with salt and pepper. We also use avocado, chopped tomato, grated cheese, and fresh cilantro for garnish.

Start by slicing the onion into fairly thick slices, so you can handle them on the grill more easily. Use bell peppers of various colors if you can find them, and slice them into rings, discarding the seeds and pith.

Grill the vegetables with the meat, turning them to get some char marks on them.

For tacos, slice the meat across the grain into strips. Sprinkle the grated cheese over the meat so it will melt a little, and stuff the tortillas with the meat and other fillings. I guarantee rave reviews with these tacos!

Or warm some flour tortillas (preferably uncooked) on a griddle until they are done and have some char specks on them, fold them, and stuff them with the meat, vegetables, garnish, and whatever salsa or hot sauce you prefer. This is also a very popular dish around here, and is the one I usually choose to make during hot weather.

I think the bottom line is that with all these good ingredients you can't go wrong. Just decide if you want corn or flour tortillas, warmed or fried, and what you want to put in them. In some cases, this is determined by what you find in the fridge.

Don't get hung up on details or trying to be too authentic. You can come up with delicious versions yourself. As to what's authentic, I see different recipes (and names) in nearly every city, both in the U.S. and Mexico. So relax and enjoy!

San Diego's Fish Tacos

We fell in love with Rubio's fish tacos way back when we first came to San Diego. Ralph Rubio had a small taco shop in Pacific Beach, which has now grown into a publicly-owned chain of restaurants.

The original recipe is said to have come from San Felipe, a small fishing village on the East coast of Baja California. Nowadays, lots of places serve fish tacos, in a variety of ways.

This recipe is from one that Rubio's published in the newspaper a long time ago. The only thing I have changed (sorry, Mr. Rubio) is the white sauce.

Rubio's original white sauce, and it's very good, is a half and half mixture of mayonnaise and plain yogurt. My family and I think my sauce is a little more exciting. I suggest you try both. We also like to use our Aioli Cayenne Sauce for fish tacos. Or make up your own.

In the photo, I've served the fish taco with guacamole, shredded cabbage, and salsa, with a piece of lime as garnish. The fish is catfish, which was great, but we also frequently use tilapia!

Here's the recipe for Fish Tacos:

1 cup mayonnaise
3 chipotle chiles, chopped
1 cup flour
1 cup beer
1/2 teaspoon salt
1 tablespoon seasoning (garlic powder, cayenne pepper, or one of your favorites)

12 filets of cod, tilapia, red snapper, halibut, catfish, or other firm white fish
Oil
12-24 corn tortillas
1 head green cabbage, shredded
Fresh cilantro, chopped
4 limes, cut into wedges

As you can see in the photo, each taco doesn't hold a very big piece of fish, so take that into account when you buy and carve up the fish. This recipe calls for deep frying the fish, but you can also fry it in a skillet, or you can grill the fish with no coating at all for a lower calorie version. You can serve each taco with one tortilla, or to make it stronger, use two tortillas per taco, as shown in the photo.

Mix the mayo and chipotles together in a small bowl.

Mix the flour, beer, salt, and seasoning in a bowl to make a thick batter. Heat the oil to 375 degrees either in the skillet or in a deep fryer. Cut the fish into pieces that will fit into the taco shell. Rinse and pat dry, dip in the batter, and fry in batches for two or three minutes until golden brown. Set aside and keep them warm. This fish is so good I also use this batter for fish and chips, sometimes with a slightly different seasoning.

Warm the corn tortillas on a griddle. Place a layer of chopped cabbage on half, top with a piece of fish, and top that with the white sauce. Fold the taco, and add some salsa and chopped cilantro. Garnish with a lime, which should be squeezed over the taco before eating. If you are also serving tortilla chips, also squeeze some lime juice over them, salt, and eat.

Go start a taco shop chain.

Multi-cooker

Use the Air Fryer feature of your Ninja Foodi or your air fryer to "fry" the fish. Now you have avoided heating a pot of oil and smelling up the place. In fact, you will find lots of Fish and Chips recipes for fried fish for your pot, both in its instruction recipe booklet or on line. You can also heat up the tortillas at the same time, in the same pot!

Chiles Rellenos de Foodi

Chiles Rellenos are really delicious, but are normally a lot of trouble, so they are kind of a special occasion dish. But the Ninja Foodi makes it so much easier that you can have them whenever you want, in half the time, and with a small fraction of the cleanup. If you don't have an air fryer or a Foodi, just follow the recipe here except fry the rellenos in ¼ " of hot oil, turning over after the bottom side browns.

Rellenos are usually fried in deep fat, after being coated with a fluffy egg batter. The chiles are stuffed with cheese most of the time, but other fillings can add variety. Use your imagination.

The main difference in the Foodi (or air fryer) method is that the uncooked rellenos need to be in a container rather than put in the fryer basket, which would leak the batter into the bottom of the pot. So I use a small casserole dish as shown in the photo above, and put the whole thing onto a rack in the pot.

Using fresh chiles, which is the best way, presents another problem. They need to be roasted and peeled, usually over an open flame. Even though I used to have a gas stove (I now have an induction range, which I like better) holding and turning the chile over the flame seemed to take forever, and was never uniform enough to make the peeling easy. And roasting in the oven took forever, ran up the utility bill, heated up the kitchen, and still they were hard to peel. So I nearly always used canned chiles.

No more! I decided that I could air fry the chiles in the Foodi, and it worked. I tried two methods: one with the chile sprayed with PAM, and the other just thrown in "as is" from the produce shelf. The one I spayed was something of a mess, but the other one was perfect! I roasted them for 12 minutes, and let them stay in the pot while they cooled enough to peel.

The unsprayed chile was also easier to handle after peeling, and held together better after stuffing. I used a stick of pepper jack string cheese after removing some of the seeds and pith through the slit in the chile.

For the batter, you need

3 eggs
3 tablespoons flour
1 teaspoon salt
1 teaspoon pepper
1/4 cup vegetable oil

Separate the eggs, putting the yolks into a small bowl and the whites into a larger one. With a beater, beat the whites until they are stiff, and then fold in the yolks and other ingredients except for the oil. Dip the stuffed chiles in the batter, and, instead of placing in hot oil, lay them in a dish that will fit in the Foodi or air fryer. Mine took about 10 minutes, but check often enough so you'll establish the time for your pot.

Shrimp Vera Cruz

Here's a delicious shrimp recipe that's fast and easy to make.

Use medium to large shrimp, and to save time and trouble, you can usually buy them peeled, de-veined, and frozen. One bag of 15-20 shrimp is enough for four servings, unless there's a hog at the table.

Serve it over rice, as shown, or in little individual casserole dishes, or even in scallop shells if you have them. The sauce is delicious, so you'll want either rice, tortillas, or bread to soak up the excess.

Here I've served the dish with refried beans and avocado slices. If you don't serve it over rice, you could also add Mexican rice as a side dish.

I fell in love with this dish at a local restaurant, and managed to get the recipe smuggled out of the kitchen by a friendly waitress one night. For historical purposes, the original is shown below written on a piece of wax paper. I've modified the recipe slightly for home cooking.

Here's how to make Shrimp Vera Cruz.

12-15 (or more) medium or large shrimp, peeled and de-veined (shells left on tail for a handle)
1 medium tomato, diced*
2 chopped green onions, or some diced regular onion*
4 tablespoons chopped fresh cilantro*
1 cup white wine
8 tablespoons (one stick) butter, cut into several pieces
2 teaspoons lemon juice
1/2 teaspoon salt
1 teaspoon Tabasco

* These ingredients are used 1/2 for the sauce and 1/2 later for garnish.

Simmer all the ingredients except the shrimp, butter, and garnish. After five minutes or so, add the shrimp and continue to simmer until the shrimp is pink, turning the shrimp once in a while. This will only take another five minutes or less. Remove the shrimp temporarily to a bowl, and whisk the butter into the sauce one piece at a time to make the sauce. After that's done, dump the shrimp back into the pan, cover it to keep warm, turn off the heat, and get ready to serve.

To be authentic, serve this with white wine or Mexican beer. Warm tortillas and Mexican Rice on the side will help soak up the yummy sauce.

Chicken Loco

    This grilled chicken recipe came about as I was trying to come close to the flavor of Pollo Loco's grilled chicken. It's citrus-based, like theirs, but not quite the same. I have a hunch their recipe is simpler, but what the heck, this recipe turned out so good I may stop trying to improve it. It certainly has been a big hit with the eaters around here.

    One of the ingredients I use is annatto (achiote); a spice that not only provides flavor but also color. If you can't find it, make this anyway; this chicken was plenty good before I added the annato.

    I found the annatto in a plastic bag on a supermarket pegboard with other Latin American spices and herbs. You need to grind up the seeds, and they are pretty hard. A spice grinder would be handy here (I used my little Magic Bullet).

    Everyone seems to know (or think) that the Pollo Loco recipe is based on pineapple juice. But since it's from Mexico, I can't help but think there's lime juice in there as well. Anyhow, this is good.

Here's how you make Chicken Loco:

2 chickens, quartered
6 ounces pineapple juice
5 ounces orange juice
2 tablespoons lime juice
2 tablespoons oil
6 tablespoons apple cider vinegar
1 teaspoon black pepper
1 teaspoon white pepper
1 tablespoon cumin
1 tablespoon garlic powder
1 tablespoon chili powder

1 teaspoon oregano
1 teaspoon poultry seasoning
1 teaspoon salt
1 teaspoon ground annato (achiote)

Pineapple juice comes in little 6-ounce cans, which I keep on hand for cooking. That's where the 6 ounces came from. Five ounces is half a little plastic bottle of un-refrigerated orange juice, which I also keep on hand, and I figured 10 ounces was too much, so I drank half of it.

Quarter the chickens, rinse them off, and set them aside. Mix all the other ingredients and pour into one or more plastic bags and add the chicken. Massage a little, and let marinate for 1/2 hour to a day or more, in the fridge.

When it's time to cook, remove the chicken from the marinade, save a little for basting, and discard the rest. Grill the chicken over medium coals (or gas flame) for 40 -45 minutes, until the legs move freely, juice from the thigh runs clear, or the internal temperature gets up to 170 degrees F. Turn the chicken every ten minutes or so during this period, and also move the pieces around so they cook as uniformly as possible. You can baste the chicken with the marinade for the first 30 minutes, but the basting liquid must have time to cook. It's been in the raw chicken, you know.

A few flare-ups are OK, and add flavor to the meat. If the flare-ups come up past the chicken and it's obviously going to turn the chicken to charcoal, move the chicken to a cooler part of the grill, and maybe use a spray bottle to water down the flames a bit. Grilling slow and steady is best.

Serve with Cole slaw, refried beans, corn on the cob or whatever else you like. As I said, everyone so far has loved the flavor of this chicken!

About the Author

Mr. Choisser received his degree in electrical engineering at the University of Arizona, and took graduate courses in mathematics at Syracuse University. He is an Air Force veteran, having been an officer in the Data Processing Branch of the Intelligence and Electronic Warfare Directorate of Rome Air Development Center, Griffiss AFB, New York. Upon leaving the service, he was awarded the Air Force Systems Command Award for Scientific Achievement. In his business career, his work involved the development of low-light-level sensors for military and scientific uses. He is one of the co-inventors and developer of the Digicon, the multi-channel photon counting image tubes used in both of the original Hubble Space Telescope spectrographs. He was awarded special recognition for this work by the NASA Goddard Space Flight Center. His longest career was designing and building industrial versions of the IBM PC. An early project was with Teledyne Ryan, helping with the design of the cockpit data recorder for the Boeing 747. His subsequent work with industry and the military resulted in the use of Microsoft DOS and Windows in a wide variety of non-desktop applications. He was editor-in-chief of the Windows CE Tech Journal, a Miller-Freeman publication. His hobbies have always been airplanes, gardening, cooking, and golf. Writing has been a life-long pursuit, now more for pleasure than for business. Today his books involve cooking, aquaponics, and books intended to induce curiosity and wonder in young people about math, science, and engineering.

Prologue

This book is finished, and I think I'll go have a marguerita. One of the beauties of publishing today either by eBook or print-on-demand is that if you or I find mistakes or additions that are necessary, I can make them practically instantly. That takes a lot of tension out of publishing. In my past publishing career, months of work would go into technical books that were bound to have some errors, and we were constantly publishing errata notices out to the engineering community in spite of losing sleep over the editing and proof reading. I like cooking better, because a little mistake won't keep your computer from booting!

Let me know how you like this book. Here's wishing you good health, good cooking, and delightful eating!

John, the Cooking Dude

www.cookingdude.com

www.cookingdude.com

Made in the USA
San Bernardino, CA
28 April 2019